Auroville

A DREAM TAKES SHAPE

AF080790

A Dream Take Shape (English)
Copyright : Prisma, Auroville
Author : Franz Fassbender
Photographs : John Mandeen

First edition: 2023

ISBN 978-93-95460-44-6 (Paperpack)
ISBN 978-93-95460-52-1 (ebook)

BISAC Code:
HIS062000, HISTORY / Asia / South / India
HIS037070, HISTORY / Modern / 20th Century / General
HIS003000, History / Asia / General
HIS030000, HISTORY / Reference

Thema Subject Category:
2ACG, German
JBS, Social groups, communities and identities
NH, History
NHF, Asian history
NHT, History: specific events and topics
NHTB, Social and cultural history

Cataloging-in-Publication Data for this title is available from the Library of Congress.

Published by:
PRISMA, an imprint of Digital Media Initiatives
PRISMA, Aurelec / Prayogshala,
Auroville 605101, Tamil Nadu, India

www.prisma.haus

Auroville charter

On 28 February 1968, inauguration day and first reading of Auroville's 4-point Charter

1. *Auroville belongs to nobody in particular. Auroville belongs to humanity as a whole. But to live in Auroville one must be a willing servitor of the Divine Consciousness.*

2. *Auroville will be the place of an unending education, of constant progress and a youth that never ages.*

3. *Auroville wants to be the bridge between the past and the future. Taking advantage of all discoveries from without and from within, Auroville will boldly spring towards future realisations.*

4. *Auroville will be a site of material and spiritual researches for a living embodiment of an actual Human Unity.*

a dream

In 1954, The Mother wrote the following text.
It was originally meant for the Sri Aurobindo Ashram,
where she saw a practical ground to implement this vision.
In 1965, The Mother decided to launch the project of Auroville,
to continue manifesting the 'Dream' on a wider platform.

A Dream: There should be somewhere upon earth a place that no nation could claim as its sole property, a place where all human beings of good will, sincere in their aspiration, could live freely as citizens of the world, obeying one single authority, that of the supreme Truth; a place of peace, concord, harmony, where all the fighting instincts of man would be used exclusively to conquer the causes of his suffering and misery, to surmount his weakness and ignorance, to triumph over his limitations and incapacities; a place where the needs of the spirit and the care for progress would get precedence over the satisfaction of desires and passions, the seeking for pleasures and material enjoyment.

In this place, children would be able to grow and develop integrally without losing contact with their soul. Education would be given, not with a view to passing examinations and getting certificates and posts, but for enriching the existing faculties and bringing forth new ones. In this place, titles and positions would be supplanted by opportunities to serve and organise.

The needs of the body will be provided for equally in the case of each and every one. In the general organisation intellectual, moral and spiritual superiority will find expression not in the enhancement of the pleasures and powers of life but in the increase of duties and responsibilities. Artistic beauty in all forms, painting, sculpture, music, literature, will be available equally to all, the opportunity to share in the joys they bring being limited solely by each one's capacities and not by one's social or financial position.

For in this ideal place money would be no more the sovereign lord. Individual merit will have a greater importance than the value due to material wealth and social position. Work would not be there as the means of gaining one's livelihood, it would be the means whereby to express oneself, develop one's capacities and possibilities, while doing at the same time service to the whole group, which on its side would provide for each one's subsistence and for the field of his work.

In brief, it would be a place where relations between human beings, usually based almost exclusively upon competition and strife, would be replaced by relations of emulation for doing better, for collaboration, relations of real brotherhood, for collaboration, relations of real brotherhood.

The earth is certainly not ready to realise such an ideal, for mankind does not yet possess the necessary knowledge to understand and accept it or the indispensable conscious force to execute it. That is why I call it a dream.

Yet, this dream is on the way to becoming a reality. That is exactly what we are seeking to do at the Sri Aurobindo Ashram on a small scale, in proportion to our modest means. The achievement is indeed far from being perfect but it is progressive: little by little we advance towards our goal which, we hope, one day we shall be able to hold up before the world as a practical and effective means of coming out of the present chaos in order to be born into a more true, more harmonious new life.

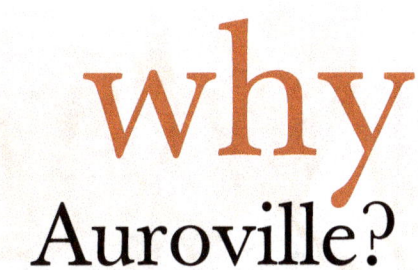

why Auroville?

Some years later, in 1969, The Mother read a passage written by one of her closest disciples, Satprem, addressed to students who sought revolution and change throughout the world.

She entitled it "Answer to Why Auroville?"

"This is the time of **the great sense**.

"We look to the right or left, we build theories, reform our Churches, invent super-machines...

"We want to improve the existent – but it is no longer the time to improve the existent: does one improve rot? – This is the time for **something else**. "Something else" is not the same thing with an improvement...

"We must look to the Great Sense...

"This is what the Great Sense says:

"It says that we were born so many millions of years ago – a molecule, a gene, a bit of quivering plasm – and we have produced a dinosaur, a crab, a monkey. And if our eyes had stopped half way along the road, we could have said, with reason(!), that the Baboon was the summit of creation, and there was nothing better to do, unless to improve our capacities of monkeyhood and to create a United Kingdom of Monkeys... And perhaps we are committing the same error today in our forest of concrete. Is man truly the end of all these millions of years of effort? – the matriculation for all and the washing machine?

"The Great Sense, the True Sense, tells us that man is not the final goal. It is not the triumph of man that we want, not an improved version of an intelligent dwarf – it is another being on the earth, another race amongst us.

"Sri Aurobindo has said: 'Man is a transitional being'. We are right in the middle of this transition, it is cracking from all sides: in Biafra, in Israel, in China, on Boul'Mich*. Man is ill at ease in his skin.

"And the Great Sense, the True Sense, tells us that the best we can do is to set to work to find the secret of the transition, the "great passage" towards the new being – as one day we found the passage from monkey to man – and to collaborate with our own evolution instead of turning in a circle and seizing false powers to govern a false life.

"But where is the lever of this transmutation?

"It is within.

"There is a Consciousness within, there is a Power within, the very one which pushed in the dinosaur, in the crab, in the monkey, in man... Instead of letting the evolution unfold through millennia of unproductive painful attempts and useless deaths and fake revolutions that revolutionize nothing, we can shorten the time, we can make a concentrated evolution – we can be conscious creators of the New Being.

"In truth, it is the time of the Great Adventure. The adventure is within – freedom is within, space is within, and the transformation of our world by the power of the Spirit. Because, indeed, this Power was always there, supreme, all-powerful, pushing the evolution forward: this was the hidden Spirit which grows to become the Spirit manifest upon the earth, and if we have confidence, if we want the supreme Power, if we have the courage to descend into our hearts, everything is possible, because God is in us."

* The boulevard in front of the Sorbonne in Paris, France, where in May 1968 a student revolt broke out.

the original plan
with the four zones

Auroville wants to be a universal township where men and women of all countries are able to live in peace and progressive harmony, above all creeds, all politics and all nationalities.

The purpose of Auroville is to realise human unity.

The project is guided by this ideal. The overall concept of the town provides for a material focus, the Matrimandir, surrounded by four zones, the Cultural, International, Industrial and Residential.

At the centre is the Matrimandir, symbolizing *"union with the divine manifesting in a progressive human unity"*.

A **Green Belt,** a zone for environmental regeneration, afforestation, sanctuaries and organic farming, will eventually surround the entire city area.

In the **Cultural Zone** will be located the main infrastructure for an education which will not be given with a view to passing examinations, but will place emphasis on growth of the soul and the experiential perception of the inner unity connecting all human beings. This zone is also the main place for artistic, cultural and sports activities.

In the **International Zone**, the national pavilions will present in a living manner the deep unity of nations and peoples while also celebrating the diversity of their cultures. It is further planned to build there a research institute, the Centre for International Research in Human Unity (CIRHU), which will aim to become an international forum for conceiving and initiating plans of action to develop such a unity.

In the **Industrial Zone**, the place for generation of money for this intended self-supporting township, the emphasis will not be on productivity and competition (and the pressure that comes with it) but on relations of emulation for doing better.

In the **Residential Zone**, there will be low- as well as relatively high-density housing, with architectural design which facilitates easy communication and interaction between the residents.

The banyan tree and the Matrimandir, geographical centre and soul of Auroville.

The original conceptual plan of Auroville,

shown above, was conceived in 1967.

It gives, within a diameter of two and a half kilometres,

some guidelines for construction.

But it is not a rigid plan; it is evolving as the town grows, while holding

to its basic architectural principle of a galaxy shape.

It is constantly being re-examined by some

who wish to secure natural and organic growth,

and by others who favour growth within certain guidelines.

Auroville is planned to eventually accommodate

50,000 residents, a number which The Mother considered sufficient

to allow this experiment in human unity

to take on a meaningful and significant dimension.

the plan

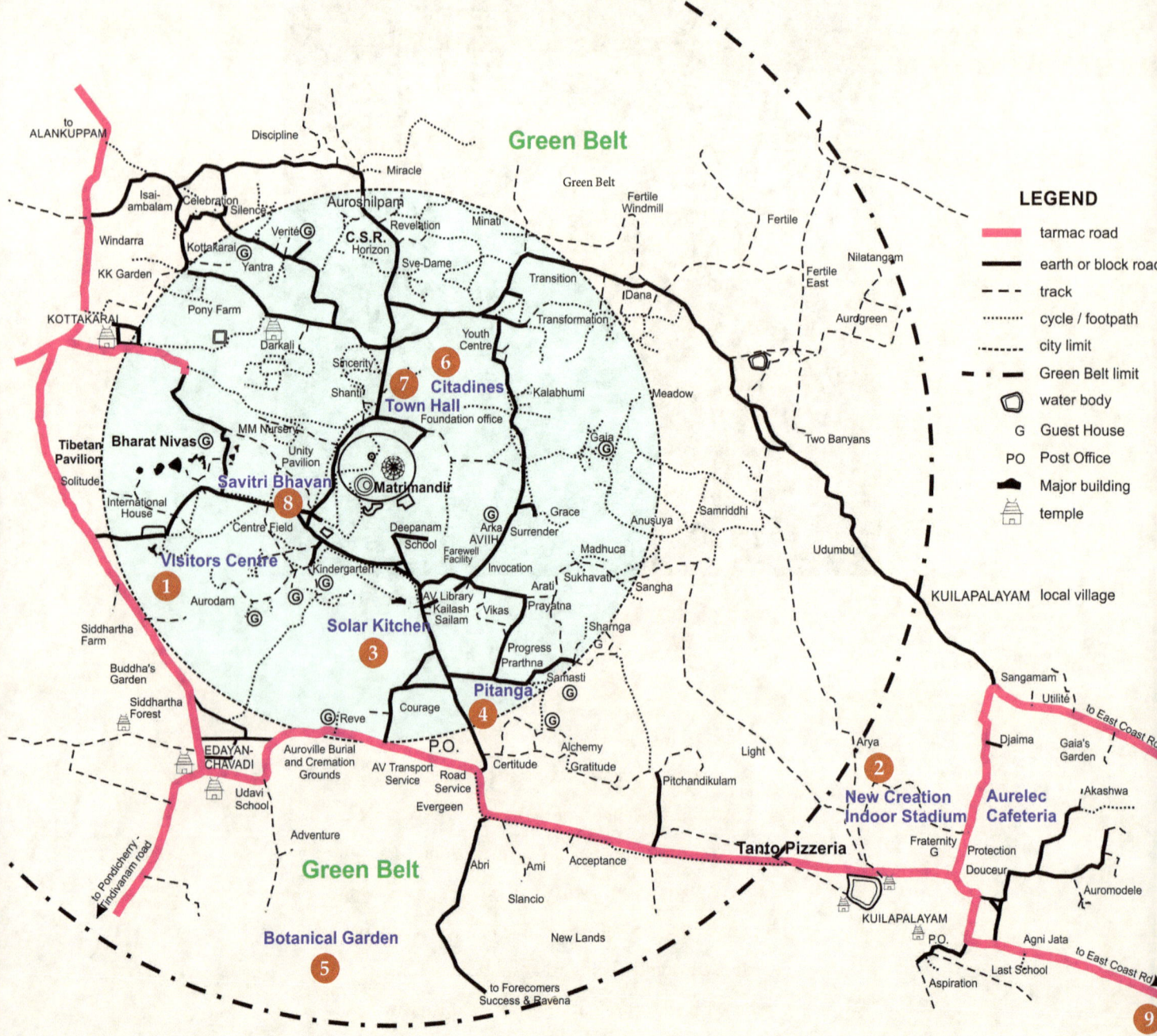

1. Visitors Centre with exhibitions, cafeteria and boutiques

2. Multipurpose Indoor Stadium at New Creation Sports Ground

3. Solar Kitchen dining hall

4. Pitanga Hall – a multi-purpose cultural complex

5. Preparing saplings for the Green Belt

6. Citadines – apartments for Aurovilians

7. Centre for Urban Research, or 'Town Hall'

8. Savitri Bhavan – for studying Sri Aurobindo's 'Savitri' and other texts

9. Quiet Healing Centre by the beach

auroville evolves

The Mother had been "dreaming" of a project like Auroville for quite some time. However, it was only in 1965 that she began to work actively on it. A French architect, Roger Anger, was given the responsibility of preparing the initial town lay-out, and worked on it with his colleagues in Paris. The purchase of land started. At that time, those interested in the project were mainly staying in Pondicherry.

The official inauguration took place on 28th February 1968, with a formal ceremony attended by some 5,000 people around a lotus bud shaped Urn, into which was placed the Auroville Charter and earth from all over India and the world as a gesture of national and global unity.

As the pioneers arrived to settle in Auroville from 1968 onwards, they initially established themselves on the outskirts of the future township, in settlements with names such as Promesse, Hope, Forecomers and Aspiration.

For several years no permanent construction was authorised on the site of the future town, except for the Matrimandir and Bharat Nivas (the Pavilion of India), the construction of which started in 1971.

The development of the project was first concentrated in the settlement of Aspiration, then in Auromodèle, an area earmarked for experimentation near the village of Kuilapalayam, in order to make a concrete attempt at learning how to live in Auroville and in the Green Belt, an area of forests, farms and nature sanctuaries planned to surround the future town.

In 1974 there were already over 320 Aurovilians. With an average yearly growth rate of 3-5% to date, the number of Aurovilians had reached over 3,000 by early 2019. Out of that number 44.5% were Indian, 14.1% French, 8.5% German, 5.5% Italian, 3.4% Dutch and in the remaining 24% there are numerous other nationalities present.

If the present trend of growth is sustained, Auroville could theoretically reach its full complement of 50,000 inhabitants within 30 years. However, there is no time schedule to achieve 50,000. Numbers have far less importance than the quality and dedication of people settling here.

Out of some 120 settlements, by no means all are in the Residential Zone of the township. They comprise a variety of dwellings ranging from simple structures to apartments and villa-style residences.

Schools for Auroville's children are found in or near five locations – Centre Field, New Creation, Transition, Transformation and Aspiration.

Two national pavilions have been completed: the Indian Pavilion named Bharat Nivas and the Pavilion of Tibetan Culture. Others are planned or being worked on, some likely to have a "temporary" nature at this point.

Around 250 commercial units, mostly doing handicrafts, are widely scattered around the township, with a higher concentration in the Industrial Zone.

Wind Generators   Solar Collector   Solar Panels

with a strong environmental emphasis

A land which has returned to life...

The land chosen to host the Auroville experiment was largely eroded, and officially described as being in an advanced state of desertification.

From the very outset, a number of Aurovilians, in collaboration with local villagers, took up the task of bringing this land back to life. There followed many years of working with nature, of struggling with the climate and with herds of cows and goats in search of food. Through consistent tree planting – mostly using indigenous species – and organic farming methods, the Aurovilians have reversed the desertification process and regenerated the land on a long term basis, at the same time building in control and harvesting features for rainwater.

These results have been obtained by constant research into how to achieve the greatest productivity without artificial fertilisers or other chemical products, using only organic methods to develop an intensive polyculture.

Over the span of 50+ years since Auroville's inauguration, this effort has resulted in the establishment of around two million forest and fruit trees on Auroville's present holding of around 3,000 acres (approx 1,215 hectares), over half of which is situated in the Green Belt, a zone for environmental regeneration, afforestation, sanctuaries and organic farming that is planned to eventually surround the entire city area. Less than 200 acres are still required to consolidate the land in the city area and around 1,700 to complete the Green Belt.

The Indian Government has recognised the value of Auroville's greenwork. Throughout the years, Aurovilians have hosted a considerable number of seminars and training schemes relating to green work in the country and have widely participated in indigenous programmes of afforestation and environmental improvement.

An increasing utilisation of renewable energy...

The generation of energy for many houses is provided by non-conventional means. Of the total of over 1,500 residential units, several hundred are running fully or partially on electricity produced by photovoltaic panels. Some 20 windmills pump water in addition to over 200 solar photovoltaic pumps, and there is a 51 KW photovoltaic power plant which provides electricity for the Matrimandir. The Solar Kitchen uses steam produced by a 15 metre diameter solar bowl concentrator (the largest in India) for cooking food. Then, on a smaller scale, many people also use solar cookers, solar water heaters and biogas units to produce energy for domestic needs.

Varuna Auroville, a registered unit under the 'For All Pour Tous Trust', now has a wind generator located in the Thiruppur District of Tamil Nadu that provides electricity directly to Auroville's high tension connections, and a second generator in Karnataka that sells energy to a third party to raise funds for Auroville. Another 3 generators are owned by Airstream, an independent registered company having 3 wind generators that by way of separate partnerships generate income annually that is donated to Auroville to help meet the cost of electricity plus energy-related expenses within the township.

In 1997, the Centre for Scientific Research (CSR) received an award for being the "Best Non-Government Organisation in India in the renewable energy sector" from the Ministry for Non-Conventional Energy Sources. In 2004, Auroville's Aurore unit won a 'Green Oscar' in the form of the a globally-significant Ashden Award for Sustainable Energy.

the matrimandir
the soul of auroville

Why Matrimandir?...

The Matrimandir wants to be the symbol of the Universal Mother, according to Sri Aurobindo's teaching.

21 February 1972: Ceremony marking the beginning of the construction of Matrimandir

The Matrimandir is a place dedicated to the Universal Mother, a concept well known in Hindu culture. For Westerners, the reason for such a building is often difficult to understand, as the Mother pointed out when an essay on the subject was presented to her for approval:

In India, for centuries the creation, that is basically the working of the creatrix Mother, has been considered as anti-divine.

Sri Aurobindo taught that it is in matter that the Divine must be manifested, and has insisted on the understanding of this notion of the creatrix Mother.

Matrimandir is to teach people that it is not by retiring from this world nor by ignoring it that they will realise the Divine during their lifetime.

I do not want it to become a religious place; there must be absolutely no dogmas, nor rules, nor rituals.

Indians, for the great majority, do not need any explanation; they understand it because of their culture. But only one Westerner out of a million will understand that such a building is necessary.

The Inner Chamber...

The Mother gave, in various talks, very accurate indications for the design, the layout, the purpose and use of the Inner Chamber, as she saw it in a vision at the beginning of 1970. Here is a selection of her statements:

It will be a kind of hall like the inside of a column, a tower with twelve facets, each facet represents a month of the year. Right in the centre on the floor is my symbol, and above it four of Sri Aurobindo's symbols joined to form a square, and above that a globe of 70 centimetres diameter.

The sun should enter as a ray, without diffusion: an arrangement must be made so that the ray of sunlight can be seen. When there is no sun (at nights and on cloudy days) lights will be lit which will have the same effect and the same colour. Right at the bottom, under the globe, there will be a light which will be directed upwards, diffusing light into the globe. It will always be in a kind of clear half-light: day and night.

Inside, there will be twelve columns, situated half-way between the centre and the walls. These will be six metres away from the centre. No windows. Ventilation with air-conditioners. On the floor, a carpet, everywhere except for the centre. Everything will be white. No flowers, no incense nor music. People can sit everywhere. Inside no talking. Silence.

One descends deep down and one comes up inside the temple again. It is a symbol. Everything is symbolic.

People will not come for a regular meditation or anything of that kind: it will be a place for concentration, for trying to find one's consciousness.

The Mother selected the outer form of the Matrimandir design from various models presented to her in March 1970.

The main structure is a flattened sphere, 36m in diameter by 29.5m high, within which is located the **Inner Chamber** visualised by The Mother.

Around the Matrimandir sphere, **Twelve Meditation Rooms** are located inside twelve "petals" which extend out to the edge of **Twelve Surrounding Gardens** radiating out from the Matrimandir. An additional garden, called the Garden of Unity, is dominated by a large **Banyan Tree**, the geographic centre of Auroville. Close by is an open **Amphitheatre** with at its focal point the **Urn** which featured in Auroville's inauguration ceremony in 1968.

Excavation for the Matrimandir foundations began in March 1971, with some Aurovilians and a number of other workers who undertook to build the Matrimandir without paid labour, putting their whole heart into it and infusing it with their consciousness. But several months later it became necessary to invite local villagers to join them on a salary basis in order to speed up the work. *The Matrimandir will be the soul of Auroville. The sooner the soul is there, the better it will be for everybody, especially for the Aurovilians,* said The Mother.

The Inner Chamber

Concerning the consciousness inside the Matrimandir, The Mother explained: *"Build it; I will make it a very strong centre, but only those who are capable will perceive it."*

One year later, in February 1972, the first load of cement was poured into the 14,000 cubic metre crater. On the 17th November 1973, at the exact time when The Mother left her body, the Aurovilians completed the concrete ring linking the four pillars which support the Matrimandir. From then on the construction continued in a very regular manner, without any halt, progressing according to the rhythm of the dedicated team of workers.

In 1994, the Inner Chamber, though not fully completed at the time, was opened to the public. The main sphere of the Matrimandir was completed in 2009, barring a few remaining details, but the gardens will take a few more years, and the planned surrounding lake considerably longer.

The general layout for the gardens area is more or less finalised, though the size of the lake and sourcing of the water needed to fill it has yet to be decided.

The Amphitheatre, fully covered with red Agra stone, is regularly used for late afternoon gatherings of a meditative nature; also as a site for a pre-dawn bonfire on Auroville's and Sri Aurobindo's birthdays.

schools

in a town dedicated to an unending education

> *Education will be based on what we hope to receive from the future, not on what we know about the past. What we want to teach is not only a mental idea, it is a new idea of life and a realisation of consciousness.*

The Cultural Zone, with its educational sub-zone, primarily focuses on educational, cultural, artistic and sports activities.

Its geographical area in the future town is well defined. Auroville's main elementary school, "Transition", as well as its high schools "Future School" and "Last School", are located there, along with a large Sports Ground, a Youth Centre, the Centre for Research in Performing Arts (CRIPA) and Kalabhoomi, a community for artists with some residential buildings and rehearsal and performance facilities.

A research in new teaching methods...

"The first principle of true teaching is that nothing can be taught," wrote Sri Aurobindo. *"The teacher is not an instructor or task-master, he is a helper and a guide. His business is to suggest and not to impose. He does not actually train the pupil's mind, he only shows him how to perfect his instruments of knowledge and helps and encourages him in the process. He does not impart knowledge to him, he shows him how to acquire knowledge for himself."*

The child must learn that *there is only one true guide, that is the inner guide, who does not pass through the mental consciousness... It is not a question, of course, of giving a child philosophical explanations, but he could very well be given the feeling of this kind of inner comfort, of satisfaction, and sometimes of an intense joy when he obeys this little very silent thing within him which will prevent him from doing what is contrary to it.*

After School   Deepanam School   Future School

The Mother was not in favour of conventional school buildings. In 1970, when some money arrived ear-marked for a "school", she named it "Last School". One year later, when another grant arrived for the building of another school, she named it "No School"!

Several schools have been built in Auroville, since this sort of establishment is still considered very convenient for the purpose of educating children. Maybe, one day, methods of teaching will be developed and implemented without formal schools, and all activities throughout Auroville will be places of learning, which will give a further dimension to this statement in the Charter: *Auroville will be the place of an unending education, of constant progress and a youth that never ages.*

A recognition of traditional educational levels...

Auroville runs two different types of schools: schools for the children of Aurovilians, and schools for the children of local villagers, whose language medium and curriculum are different. Almost all the schools for the local people, catering to around 1,200 children and students, are adjacent to their villages. Schools for Aurovilians are located mostly in the Cultural Zone or close to Aspiration settlement.

It was in Aspiration that the principle of the traditional school system was questioned not long after Auroville started, since it was understood that the Mother had indicated that education would not take place in traditional school buildings. As a consequence, the doors were closed to a whole generation of children, who didn't attend formal classes for several years. The way the experiment was then conducted was not considered fruitful, however, and was later abandoned, not least because of the need expressed by the children themselves.

A centralised structure...

The foundation of the **Sri Aurobindo International Institute of Educational Research** (SAIIER) in 1984, which now coordinates all programmes of education in Auroville, has resulted in the creation of an administrative and financial support system for education.

Presently the teachers offer to some 540 children and students studying in Auroville's schools the possibility of reaching – without examinations or diplomas – the Indian 12th standard level.

The education of children begins in Auroville's two crèches, one located behind Deepanam School, the other, Nandanam, in Centre Field area. Both are places where Auroville's youngest children can learn several languages in a natural way. When they get older, they go on to join the **Kindergarten** in Centre Field, set in beautiful surroundings with two playgrounds and two small swimming pools.

The Kindergarten provides an ideal educational environment for young children

Around the age of seven, the children then join a primary school, usually Transition School (1st through 8th grades) or Deepanam (1st through 6th grades).

The academic equivalent of the higher secondary level – 9th to 12th standards in the Indian system – can be pursued in three schools. Those who wish to explore a Free Progress education and who are not interested in exams or certificates can attend Last School. Those who definitely wish to pursue advanced studies in India, and need to pass Indian exams, can join New Era Secondary School, Udavi School or Kuyilapalayam Trust School. There is also the possibility of pursuing vocational training programmes at the Auroville Institute of Applied Technology. The third option at this level is Future School, where students can choose to prepare for external 'O' and 'A' level exams. A final possibility is to follow correspondence courses.

For a still village-size community of just under 3,500 inhabitants at the time of printing, Auroville offers an exceptional educational experience (with very few outside teachers), but it is still striving towards further implementation of its ideals.

Resident parents are financially responsible for those children who wish to study outside, as the educational system of Auroville does not yet provide scholarships. A number of them study at the secondary level in traditional schools in nearby Pondicherry (French medium).

Regular sports and physical education activities...

Sports activities are central to Auroville's vision and take place mainly in the sports complex in the Cultural Zone, where one can find football, basketball, handball, a running track and other facilities. Six tennis courts are in use daily, located in several places. Horse-back riding is also a regular possibility.

...and also cultural activities.

Pitanga Hall (at Samasti settlement) offers dance, hatha-yoga and a variety of body-awareness activities. It is also available to Auroville artists for exhibitions of their work and for occasional cultural events.

Music programmes, choir performances, recitals, etc, take place in the Centre for Research in Performing Arts (CRIPA), Pitanga Hall, or occasionally in Vérité settlement. Major dance programmes, often with renowned visiting artists, and theatre plays take place mostly in the Sri Aurobindo Auditorium at Bharat Nivas. The "Savitri Bhavan" complex hosts regular classes and lectures on Savitri, the epic 24,000 line poem by Sri Aurobindo.

national pavilions

expressing the soul of each nation or culture

The International Zone is planned to be like an international campus, emphasizing in a living manner by way of national pavilions the human unity between people of different races, religious backgrounds and cultures. Here, a nation or a group of nations with a well defined culture will have a home in a pavilion where its place in the concert of nations will be shown in a concrete way.

The Unity Pavilion

Before the national pavilions are ready, each pavilion group will have the opportunity to be inspired by the vision of the International Zone through involvement in the activities of the 'Unity Pavilion'. Located on the future Crown Road surrounding the inner city, this pavilion aims to help promote understanding between peoples and cultures in such a way as to facilitate and speed up development of the International Zone as a whole, by focusing on topics such as human unity, world peace, east-west and north-south relations, sustainable development and human potential. It aims to specifically participate in research towards finding "the soul" of each nation and its "dharma" – its true work and role as a part of the development of humanity and the evolution of life on earth.

As visualised by the Mother, the pavilions will have to play four major roles.

The pavilion, a place to highlight manifestations of the soul of a nation...

Even as the individual has a psychic being which is the true self, governing more or less openly his or her destiny, so too each nation has its psychic being which is its true self, molding its destiny behind a veil. It is the soul of the country, the national genius, the spirit of the people, the centre of national aspiration, the fountain-head of all that is beautiful, noble, great and generous as a tangible reality...

The specificity of each nation may be recognized more easily during its great historic moments, when its psychic being was pre-eminent and was playing a role in its evolution, as well as, at times, in the evolution of mankind.

Each nation has to occupy its own place and fulfil its role in the world concert. This must not be understood as meaning that each nation would choose its place arbitrarily, through its ambition and its greed. A country's mission is not a thing to be settled mentally, with all the egoistic and ignorant preferences of the external consciousness, because that would serve only to shift the field of the conflict between nations, but the conflict would continue, perhaps in a more accentuated form...

India's role is to be the spiritual heart of the terrestrial body just as, for example, the role of Germany is to express skill, or that of Russia the brotherhood of man, or that of the United States' enthusiasm for adventure and practical organisation, or that of France's generosity of sentiment, newness and boldness of ideas and chivalry in action...

The pavilion, a place for events...

... not with a commercial aim, but with a view to showing the genius of each country, how it has expressed itself in the past, its mission in the world concert, how it has participated in the evolution of mankind, and what is its cultural, philosophical and industrial contribution to the world.

The culture of the different regions of the Earth will be represented here in such a way as to be accessible to all, not merely intellectually in ideas, theories, principles and languages, but also vitally in habits and customs, in art in all forms – painting, sculpture, music, decoration – and physically too through natural scenery, dress, games, sports, industries and food. A kind of world-exhibition has to be organized in which all countries will be represented in a concrete and living manner.

The pavilion, a place for education...

The best education that can be given to children consists in teaching them what the true nature of their country is and its own qualities, the mission their nation is to fulfil in the world and its true place in the terrestrial concert. To that should be added a wide understanding of the role of other nations, but without the spirit of imitation and without ever losing sight of the genius of one's own country... so that they may know and respect equally the true spirit of all the countries upon earth.

To make this possible, children from a very early age must be accustomed not merely to the idea but also to its practice. Therefore the international area will be international not because students from all countries will be admitted here, not because education will be given in their own mother tongue, but particularly because the culture of the different regions of the earth will be represented here.

A lodging house could be attached where students of the same nationality would be accommodated. They would thus enjoy the culture of their motherland and at the same time receive the education which can introduce them to other cultures of the Earth.

The Mother indicated that four languages would be taught in Auroville: English, Tamil, French and simplified Sanskrit. The learning of other languages will be possible in linguistic laboratories of individual pavilions.

The 560 seat Sri Aurobindo Auditorium at Bharat Nivas, the Indian Pavilion

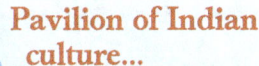

The pavilion, a meeting place for compatriots...

In future, when individuals decide to leave their country to join Auroville, their national pavilion in the International Zone will allow them to remain in contact with their own culture and will allow their Auroville-born children to also get acquainted with it.

This is why it is thought that governments of each country should take active part in the building and maintenance of pavilions, not only to show to the world their own culture, but also as a centre for their nationals, whether residents or visitors to Auroville.

The ideal is that every nation with a definite culture will have a pavilion representing that culture. Each nation would find a practical and concrete interest in cultural synthesis and collaborate in the work by taking charge of the pavilion that represents it.

Some help could also come from UNESCO, which in 1966, 1968, 1970 and 1983 unanimously adopted resolutions in support of the Auroville project, moved by the Government of India. They invited all the Member States to support the project on account of its cultural and human values, which they saw as corresponding to man's physical and spiritual needs.

The concept of the national pavilions has so far been only minimally implemented, mainly on account of lack of funds and lack of a proper infrastructure. The general layout has been decided and various groupings of residents of different cultures are, in collaboration with their countries and Auroville International Centres, well on the way towards developing design patters, funding approach and meaning full content of their future pavilion.

Pavilion of Indian culture...

The building of the Indian pavilion, Bharat Nivas, started in 1971, thanks to funds being received from the Central Government and several Indian States. An architect from Madras, Mr Chakrapani, won a national competition with his design for the pavilion. In times that Auroville did not yet have a Town Hall and other administrative centres, Bharat Nivas offered its many spaces for this important work, while its open Sri Aurobindo World Centre for Human Unity (SAWCHU) functioned as venue for the community's collective meetings. Currently, its Sri Aurobindo Auditorium, Kalakendra and Bhumika Hall's spaces are widely used for high class performances, exhibitions, lectures and the like.

Other pavilions...

In 1993, the Dalai Lama laid the foundation stone of the Pavilion of Tibetan Culture, which was completed and inaugurated by His Holiness in January 2009 and hosts many activities throughout the year. In still more rudimentary form also the African Pavilion came off the ground, while an US-oriented International House serves as guesthouse in the zone. Foundation stones have been laid for the French Pavilion by the French Ambassador and for the German and Russian Pavilions by their respective Consuls. In the areas of the future French and European Pavilions, simple temporary structures have come up, in which activities pertaining to those nations are taking place. Groups of Aurovilian residents of countries such as Germany, Spain, Italy, the Americas, former USSR nations, South East Asia, South Korea, Japan and China, are in the process of planning future designs, fundraising activities and performance activities in the framework of their cultures.

residences
without ownership rights

*Auroville belongs
to nobody in particular,
it is written in the Charter, and The Mother has added:
In Auroville, nothing belongs to anyone in particular.
It is the ideal place for those who want to know the joy
and the liberation of not having personal possessions anymore.
All is collective property.*

No property rights regarding residences...

In Auroville the land and other immovable assets (houses, apartments, production units, infrastructure) do not belong to residents but are part of the collective assets of Auroville. Thus those who have money and finance houses or apartments do not own them, but have only a preferential right to occupy them. If, for some reason, they leave Auroville, they cannot sell them. Usually, they put their house at the disposal of Auroville's Housing Service, while keeping their right to preferential occupation in case they come back within a reasonable time. Other things such as cars, motorcycles, furniture, etc, still remain personal property.

Because of a lack of finances, Auroville has not yet been in a position to construct houses which would be put freely at the disposal of new arrivals. Most of the existing residences have been financed and constructed by individual Aurovilians. Some 60 or more of them are put at the disposal of Newcomers for a maximum period of two years, during which time they have to find more permanent accommodation.

From huts to individual houses and apartments...

The first Aurovilians lived in temporary structures, often roofed with coconut leaf thatch, generally in small settlements spread out over the area of the future town and its Green Belt. At Aspiration, a group of huts with a common kitchen was built to welcome twenty Aurovilians who arrived in a caravan of vehicles in 1969. This was the real start of Auroville. This community still exists, and continues to house around 50 adults today, plus their children.

For many years, inexpensive thatched houses were popular, but progressively

Swayam residence

Maitreye Mitra Youth Hostel Kalpana apartments

houses using more permanent wall and roofing materials appeared. Presently a definite trend encourages apartments and row houses, which are being developed in a number of communities in the Residential Zone.

Over the years some 25 Auroville architects have been experimenting in housing, often in tradition-breaking ways, which explains the great diversity of styles.

An Auroville service, the **Land Board,** coordinates the purchase of land. Today within the city area, represented by a circle of about 2.5 kilometres diameter, more than three-quarters of the land belongs to Auroville; the rest belongs to local people, to temples, and to the Government. In the Green Belt, less than half of the land belongs to Auroville.

Auroville Town Development Council (ATDC), formerly L'Avenir d'Auroville, defines the general layout of the future town and prepares maps accordingly, coordinates development, and is the official body that gives permission to build, usually after receiving positive response from others in the immediate area.

A Solar Kitchen caters for Aurovilians and their guests...

but not to the needs of casual day visitors (as cash payment is not accepted). The latter can take meals, however, in places like the Visitors Centre Cafeteria, Aurelec Cafeteria, Tanto Pizzeria, Naturellement Garden Caf in Sve Dame, and a number of other venues within the Auroville area.

The all-Auroville community kitchen, known as the "Solar Kitchen", with its seating capacity for nearly 400 people, is presently preparing up to 1,100 lunches daily. One third are served in the common dining-room, the rest are distributed to Auroville schools, work places and settlements. The Solar Kitchen is like a living heart to Auroville, where Aurovilians, Newcomers and guests, normally scattered over a large area, can meet and interact daily in a lively environment.

A few communities, such as Aspiration, Vérité and Citadines, also have community kitchens, where food is prepared for their own residents.

Domestic help is often present...

Most of the houses employ a local person on a private basis to help with their cleaning and/or garden maintenance; a few also for cooking.

In this phase of Auroville's development, the contribution of local people is considered essential. It also provides village people with more attractive and more regular work than the very seasonal field work they were previously limited to; improves their financial situation; gives them access to Auroville-managed educational facilities; and generally helps widen their horizons beyond the issues dominating their lives in the local villages. Some 5,000 people, a number of whom come daily from Pondicherry, are employed in this way.

an organisation
to be based on intuitive intelligence

The Mother has given some indications about the way a system of government in Auroville would be constituted.

The first thing that all must accept and recognize is that the invisible and higher power (that is to say, which belongs to a plane of consciousness veiled for most people)... is capable of governing material things in a much more true way, much more happy, much more salutary for all, than any material power...

It is not a thing that one can pretend having... either one has it or one doesn't, because, on any occasion, if it is a pretension it will become evident...

The second thing is the power of conviction. That is to say, the highest consciousness, put in contact with matter, has spontaneously a power of conviction greater than all the intermediary regions. Its power of conviction, that is to say, its power of transformation, through simple contact, is greater than that of all the intermediary regions...

It is only what is at the very top, with a perfect purity, that has this power of spontaneous conviction. Therefore all that one can do to replace that is an approximation, and it is not much better than democracy: that is to say, the system that wants to govern by the greatest number, which often means from the lowest level.

If the representative of the Supreme Consciousness is not there... one can perhaps replace that (it should be tried) by the government of a small number – one should decide between four and eight... with an intuitive intelligence. 'Intuitive' is more important than 'intelligence': an intuition expressed intellectually. That would have inconveniences from the practical point of view, but it would perhaps be nearer the truth than anything below...

It is necessary that all who participate in the experiment must be absolutely convinced that the highest consciousness is the best judge of the most material things.

What has ruined India is the idea that the higher consciousness deals with higher things and that the things here below do not interest it at all and it understands nothing of that matter...

With that, a new type of government may be tried.

The extreme difficulty of agreeing on the selection of four to eight Aurovilians with an apparent 'intuitive intelligence' explains why this type of governance has not yet been tried, and is presently replaced by a system based on consensus within various committees and working groups.

the "Auroville Foundation"
the structure

A beginning under The Mother's guidance...

Auroville was legally started as a project of a charitable organisation, the Sri Aurobindo Society in Pondicherry, which was earlier created to diffuse Sri Aurobindo's thought and raise funds for the Ashram, while remaining an entity completely independent of the Ashram. During the early years of Auroville, the inspiration as well as the real control rested in The Mother. She was at first assisted by the Administrative Committee of Auroville, which consisted of twelve members, then by a body of four people whom she selected, then by a secretary she met every day for information and advice.

...followed by a dispute...

After The Mother left her body in 1973, the Sri Aurobindo Society insisted on keeping the financial management of the project, even though it was little involved in day-to-day development. This soon met with opposition from a majority of Aurovilians living on the land of Auroville, who felt that the spirit of the Charter given to the township by The Mother was not being respected. The outcome was that they sought to make Auroville legally independent.

...settled by the Indian Government...

Following a specific request by a majority of Auroville residents that the Government of India take over responsibility for the Auroville project, in 1980 the Indian Parliament passed a temporary resolution to this effect. Finally in 1988 it created a unique status for Auroville by passing the 'Auroville Foundation Act 1988', which established three authorities for ongoing development of the township:

- **Governing Board:** normally composed of seven persons, who are nominated and appointed for four years by the Indian Government. The Board is responsible to the Government of India for ensuring the proper functioning of the township. The Secretary to the Board lives and works full-time in Auroville, from the Auroville Foundation near the Town Hall. The Board usually meets twice a year in Auroville.

- **International Advisory Council:** comprising not more than five members of international standing who are concerned with the ideals of human unity,

Governing Board meeting at Unity Pavilion

peace and progress. The role of the Council is to advise the Governing Board on matters relating to management and development of the township, as and when required. The Council is also nominated for four years by the Indian Government.

- **Residents Assembly:** comprising all adult residents on the Auroville Master List. This body selects from its members a Working Committee of seven members which is the legal representative of the Residents Assembly, and therefore acts as the official contact body between Auroville and the Governing Board, the International Advisory Council, and the outside world in general.

The last legal body is the **Funds and Assets Management Committee** (FAMC), composed of representatives from the community plus, ex-officio, the Secretary and Under Secretary of the Auroville Foundation.

Only the Residents Assembly can take decisions which affect the whole community.

Aurovilians are trying to develop their own internal and independent organisation in such a way that the legal Government organisation need eventually only act as a supervisory body.

an internal organisation through working groups

As Auroville is a non-hierarchical society, with no management structure such as one normally sees elsewhere in the world, committees and groups take care of implementing the guidelines on Auroville and its day to day administration... As Auroville's internal organisation is constantly evolving, only its main and most permanent institutions are touched on here.

The affairs of Auroville are managed by a number of working groups which are appointed by the Residents Assembly and act in its name. There are the two statutory bodies mentioned earlier, the Working Committee and FAMC, but also the following internal bodies:

● **Auroville Council**, which deals mostly with internal matters such as the decision-making process, reorganisation,

● **Budget Coordination Committee** (BCC), which allocates a budget to those services of Auroville which are not self-supporting, and manages the resources of the central "City Services" fund to meet this budget,

● The **Auroville Town Development Council (ATDC)** formerly L'Avenir d'Auroville, a planning and coordination group which oversees Auroville's future development,

● **Housing Service**, which allocates whatever accommodation becomes available, and provides for its repair and maintenance as needed.

The above groups are housed in the Auroville Centre for Urban Research, or Town Hall, an imposing building located just to the north of Matrimandir, which was partly financed by the Asia Urbs Programme – an EC funded initiative to promote urban development through decentralised cooperation.

Once an applicant is accepted by the **Entry Board**, the decision is made known in the weekly "News & Notes". If there are no valid objections from Aurovilians within four weeks, the person is accepted. If there is a wish to build a house the individual concerned will contact the Housing Service and ATDC to know where he or she may build, or may join some collective housing scheme.

The final approval for construction of a residence is given by ATDC. This will usually be based on a satisfactory plan / design drawn up by one of the twenty five or so resident Auroville architects.

Environmental matters, particularly those related to the Green Belt, are mostly dealt with by the **Green Group**, in collaboration with the **Forest** and **Farm Groups**. Meanwhile, projects bringing general benefit to the local villages are taken care of by the **Auroville Village Action Trust**.

Food and other basic needs for daily life may be obtained from **Pour Tous Purchasing Service**, which runs a store near Aspiration, or from **Pour Tous Distribution Centre**, a second facility adjacent to the Solar Kitchen.

A job availability service is operated by the **Small Employers Welfare Administration (SEWA)** for local people seeking employment opportunities in Auroville.

If we see Auroville as presently being like a large village of nearly 3,500 inhabitants, which daily receives almost double that number of workers from the neighbouring villages, the number of activities which have already developed is quite astonishing. In fact, it must be difficult to find on Earth any other place where all the activities of an emerging township are being set up and monitored by such a small number of people.

The Auroville internal organisation has been evolving steadily over the years, and will certainly continue to do so for the foreseeable future.

an economy
to be based on exchange of services

An attempt to avoid exchange of money...
The Mother envisaged that money would not be used inside Auroville, and that only with the outside world would Auroville have monetary relations.

In fact, this original idea of no monetary exchange within the township has not been achieved to date. In spite of several attempts over the years to develop such a collective economy, money is still circulating. However, education, health care, culture and sports activities are freely available.

As the residents of Auroville are "honorary voluntary workers", Aurovilians working full-time in commercial or service units cannot receive "wages", but receive a monthly "maintenance" which is just sufficient to meet their most basic needs. This is credited to an account maintained by the **Financial Service**. Individual accounts are debited for purchases made in the two provision stores, located near Aspiration settlement and the Solar Kitchen; for various bills (electricity, telephone, etc); for payment in restaurants and cafeterias; and for cash withdrawals.

Even taking into account free housing, education, basic medical services, sports and cultural events, and the low cost of most basic commodities, it is difficult to stay in Auroville without some external financial resources, support from one's family, or help from Auroville's Unity Fund.

Meanwhile, attempts are being made to provide goods and services without exchange of money via **Prosperity Pour Tous; Nandini,** which distributes to its members new clothes received mainly from Auroville units; and a **Free Store**, which receives, repairs and distributes free second-hand items.

Finances managed with great prudence...

Each unit or service, whether it be concerned with production, construction (Matrimandir, residences or production units), environmental development (afforestation) or education, operates in a financially independent manner.

Running expenses related to the community services of Auroville are channeled through a **City Services Fund**, which is managed by the BCC. At present almost half its receipts are provided by contributions from the different commercial units, which are expected to donate a minimum of one third of their profits to the community. The other half comes from:

• individual Aurovilians and Newcomers, who contribute a monthly sum (currently Rs. 3,470 or around US$47) to sustain collective services.

• Guests, who are requested to contribute Rs. 150 for each day spent in Auroville, and Guest Houses, which are expected to contribute 20% of their income.

• interest received from funds deposited by business units or individuals in the Unity Fund.

• a percentage levied for processing project monies.

The Indian Government allocates yearly a grant which is used to cover part of the expenses of a number of units involved in education, planning, cultural and outreach activities. It has also given grants for the building of schools, a health centre, the Indian pavilion, afforestation and land reclamation, and to meet various other needs.

Money is also received from abroad, either from funding agencies or from individuals, often through the channel of Auroville International Centres.

The City Services Fund doesn't borrow any money, nor undertake building activities. Expenses and receipts are balanced each month.

money generating units
for an intended self-supporting town

Auroville aspires to be "self-supporting", which implies generating sufficient funds to meet all its own financial needs. This is likely to be done primarily through the Industrial Zone.

An organic agriculture to supply healthy food...

Farms supply organic food at cost price to the community through their FoodLink services and sell any surplus outside. They avoid use of chemical fertilisers and pesticides, for environmental and health reasons. Currently there quite a number of Auroville farms in operation, the principal ones located in the communities of Aurogreen, Revelation, Discipline, Siddhartha, Solitude, Annapurna and Auro-Orchard, with the Auroville Sustenance Farm as the most recent one. Although they make a useful contribution towards Auroville's food needs, their production is still far from sufficient to meet the full needs of the township. Apart from the Auroville Bakery, several other bakeries provide the community with all its bread needs, cakes and biscuits. Other food processing units are manufacturing jams, pickles, cheese, spreads, tofu, muesli, fruit syrups and many other such products.

Manufacturing activities creating an Aurovilian identity...

An Industrial Zone has been defined in the Master Plan for manufacturing activities. Presently there are some fifty units settled there, including Auroville Energy Products (assembling electronic equipment), Shradhanjali (flower cards and letter pads), Sunlit Future (solar power, UPS systems, etc), Mantra Pottery, the Centre for Scientific Research (CSR), the Kinisi electric mobility research & store, and the Auroville Earth Institute, offering advice and supervision on structures in compressed earth elements. Two haute couture units, Miniature and Upasana, offer high class clothing items and accessories. Much of the produce can be obtained via the Auroville Online store whose office is also located in the Zone.

Four other major units i.e. Aureka (a metalworking workshop), Auroville Press (offset printing), Auroville Papers (hand-made stationery) and Maroma (incense sticks, candles, soaps, natural body care products and perfumes) are located in the Aspiration area.

In addition to the above, there are many other units scattered around the township, ranging from architectural services to handicrafts, from food processing to garment manufacture, IT and other consultancies. Skilled and highly creative residents manufacture a wide variety of artistic products known for their fine and first-rate perfection that are mainly sold in three boutiques at the Visitors Centre and several outlets in Pondicherry town. All these units are managed by Aurovilians, who train and employ local people, thereby enabling them to better understand Auroville, together with its aims and ideals.

concern

for the surrounding villages

There are 14 villages in the immediate area of Auroville, with a combined population of around 40,000 people. More than 500 village people have joined Auroville, and there are now many young adults who were born in the villages participating fully in the life of the community.

Auroville has several centres providing education and meeting other needs for the villagers.

New Creation, for example, has established a small community with educational facilities for around 300 village children (some 50 of whom receive board and lodging) and training centres for young people in wood-work, tailoring, metal work and computers. They have also created an adjacent sports New Creation Stadium, and there is a swimming pool La Piscine.

Auroville Village Action Trust (AVAT) promotes rural development, particularly focussing on social training programmes, community organisation, women's social and economic empowerment, and supplementing primary education in village schools. In all its activities, it promotes gender and caste equality, and has facilitated developmental work in around 60 villages, benefitting approximately 5,000 people directly and around 100,000 indirectly. AVAT runs a successful micro-credit scheme leading to income-generating ventures for some 4,500 women.

Auroville Institute of Applied Technology (AIAT) is a training centre for young people from the surrounding villages, designed to help them find better employment opportunities.

The Auroville Health Centre with its doctors & nurses, diagnostic laboratory, and pharmacy attends to nearly 100 villagers every day at its headquarters near Aspiration settlement and via its 7 sub-centres. It also has on site Deepam, a unit catering to children from the local area with special needs.

Santé, Auroville's Institute for Integral Health located on the Crown Road provides consultative allopathic, ayurvedic and homeopathic health care plus acupuncture, wound dressing and health test services, mostly for Aurovilians and Newcomers, but in the case of doctor consultations also for guests subject to payment. A fully equipped ambulance available 24/7 for emergency cases is also based there.

Auroville Dental Centre and **Linea Dental Lab** take care of the dental needs of Aurovilians and the occasional guest. The former is also involved in attending to the residents of the villages around Auroville in a separate clinic located in the Auroville Health Centre compound, and via 10 rural sub-centres. Their are also two other Auroville clinics, Linea and Aurodent, in different locations.

...and a concern for **Alternative Healing.** Many Aurovilians are interested in alternative health treatments, like homeopathy, ayurveda, acupuncture, Reiki, etc. Down by the beach, in the Quiet settlement, there is a Healing Centre with guest-house facilities which puts emphasis on a variety of holistic therapies.

information
on the project
and its background

Comprehensive information on Auroville can be obtained from the **Visitors Centre**, situated in the International Zone by the entrance road leading to Bharat Nivas, and to a lesser extent from the **Boutique d'Auroville** in nearby Pondicherry.

The House of Mother's Agenda sells and promotes from the Savitri Bhavan complex the thirteen volumes compiled by Satprem, an early follower of The Mother, which record 23 years of her work on the transformation of the body and include many discussions on her vision of Auroville. A number of actual conversations are available on CD.

In the Auroville Centre for Urban Research, or Town Hall, is found the **Auroville Town Development Council (ADTC)**, which is closely involved in the physical development of the township. Nearby is the **Auroville Archives**. In the Surrender settlement the office of "**Auroville Today**", a monthly journal available by subscription, which provides a balanced viewpoint on what is happening in the community, as well as the office of the **Auroville Arts Services**.

To get further information outside Auroville, people can contact **Auroville International Centres or Liaison Offices** in more than 30 countries. Their addresses are given on the last page. And, of course, there is the comprehensive **Auroville website www.auroville.org**

Information is available from all these sources. Written information available includes a variety of publications on sale at the Visitors Centre, such as The Auroville Handbook and Auroville in a Nutshell, plus "The Mother on Auroville" in English, Tamil, French and Russian, the latter a compilation of written and verbal statements by her on the project. There is also a series of one-sheet foldout leaflets which give a brief introduction to various aspects of Auroville's daily life, such as education, reforestation, greenwork & farming, and joining the community.

To fully understand Auroville, it should be noted that the importance of an extended visit cannot be over-emphasised, since no verbal, visual or written description can adequately communicate the full reality of the township and the atmosphere pervading it.

The Visitors Centre, located by an entry road into Auroville, includes an Information Service, Exhibitions, Cafeteria and Coffee Shop, Bookshop and different boutiques displaying and selling the main products made in the township

visiting Auroville

For a tourist, there is not a great deal to see in Auroville apart from the Visitors Centre and Matrimandir, the latter with its adjacent Amphitheatre and surrounding gardens.

To really get acquainted with Auroville, it is necessary to spend some time in an Auroville guest house, from where one can easily travel around the township and Green Belt areas using one's own or hired transport.

There exist a number of major guest houses, the best known being at Centre Field (Center Guest House), Kottakarai (Afsanah Guest House), Bharat Nivas (Atithi Griha), Quiet, Samasti, Gaia's Garden and New Creation, all offering satisfactory accommodation, though at varying rates. In addition, another 250+ beds are available to guests in other communities, either in smaller guest houses or in some cases in picturesque huts.

Generally, there can be a shortage of accommodation in Auroville for guests during the peak period of December-March, and sometimes in July-August also, so it is advisable to make reservations well in advance with Auroville's Guest House Booking Service by accessing their website **www.aurovilleguesthouses.com**. More general guest information can be obtained by e-mailing to <guestservice@auroville.org.in>, or writing to Auroville Guest Service, Solar Kitchen, Auroville 605101, Tamil Nadu, India. Information about guest programmes can also be obtained from this service.

Considering the large number of visitors, the relatively small number of adult residents, and the work that needs to be done, one cannot expect the majority of residents to spend much time with guests and visitors. However, sincere and genuine interest will usually open doors to fruitful contact.

From Pondicherry, the Sri Aurobindo Ashram organizes daily visits to Auroville, which include the Visitors Centre. There, introductory videos can be seen on Auroville and the Matrimandir, and visits made to a photo exhibition on Auroville, a separate environmental exhibit, a panel exhibition on the International Zone, the information hall on the Matrimandir, an exhibition on The Mother and Sri Aurobindo, the Auroville Papers Bookshop, and to three boutiques displaying and selling examples of most of the handicraft items and garments made

in the township. There is also an Information Desk with adjacent displays of available literature, a cafeteria providing meals and other refreshments plus an additional dinner-only restaurant upstairs, the Dreamer's Café coffee bar, an evening-time 'Dosa Corner', and a small kiosk selling snack items and hiring out cycles for daily use.

Further to the above, it is possible to also enjoy snacks and meals in a variety of outlets around Auroville, though some of those located in the township area don't accept payment by cash. For the latter, it is necessary when staying in a guest house to have an Aurocard to facilitate payment.

For visiting the Matrimandir Viewing Point, free passes can be obtained from the Visitors Centre every day except Sunday afternoons. Visiting times may vary slightly, so to be sure it is best to check first by phoning the **Information Desk 0413-2622239**.

During the main guest season a number of "Introduction to Auroville" programmes are conducted for visitors and guests staying in Auroville. In the community of Vérité, seminars and workshops are sometimes held on topics like healing, Vipassana meditation and general development of consciousness.

For obvious reasons, Auroville schools, production units and residences cannot be included in a conducted tour, unless some special arrangement is made.

becoming
a resident of Auroville

Conditions for becoming an Aurovilian...

From the very beginning, The Mother has given the following admission criteria:

1. To be convinced of the essential unity of mankind and to have the will to collaborate for the materialisation of that unity,

2. To have the will to collaborate in all that furthers future realisations.

The material conditions will be worked out as the realisation proceeds.

Later she added: *In Auroville, simply the goodwill to make a collective experiment for the progress of humanity is sufficient to gain admittance.*

This makes it clear that it is not necessary to be an aspiring yogi or a disciple of Sri Aurobindo and the Mother in order to be admitted to Auroville, though it is important to have some aspiration to make inner progress by leading a more spiritual life, if the collectivity of Auroville is to move forward towards human unity.

Meanwhile, everyone interested in joining Auroville needs to know that the teachings of Sri Aurobindo and The Mother play a major role in the experiment, and it is imperative that they should feel in harmony with their vision concerning humanity's evolution and the ideal of human unity.

It is strongly recommended not to decide to come and live in Auroville without having first made a prolonged visit to the place, since it is only on the spot itself that people can know inwardly if Auroville is suitable for them or not.

Entry procedure...

Everyone who wants to join Auroville is required to stay first as a guest, and must apply to the **Entry Service**. If accepted, foreigners need to return to their own country with a letter of recommendation which can be presented to their local Indian Consulate to get an Entry Visa, without which one cannot become a resident of Auroville. Normally, after seeing the Entry Service, the applicant will immediately be accepted as a **Guest** for 3 months. At the end of that period there will be an interview with the **Entry Board** before being made a **Newcomer**. The Newcomer period is normally for a year following the 3-month guest period, during which time the person concerned is expected to integrate into the community through work and other forms of participation. At the end of this probation period, the Entry Service will announce, after consultation with the individual's "Mentors" and the wider community, whether or not the Newcomer can become an **Aurovilian**. If needed, the probation period may be extended.

Providing for individual needs...

Although it is expected that in the future Auroville will be in a position to freely welcome all potential new residents, regardless of their financial means, this is not yet possible, and Newcomers often find it costly to physically establish themselves.

The central Urn in the Amphitheatre, containing soils from the 124 countries plus all the states of India who participated in the Auroville inauguration

It certainly helps to have some independent source of finance when joining; likewise for one's ongoing participation in the community.

It is worth noting that, for instance, for a couple coming from a Western country, the expenses for the first three years may be well over US$ 50,000 (without taking into account the "maintenance" allowance they may receive from their working unit after becoming Aurovilian). This amount is needed to meet the cost of building and furnishing a residence, purchasing 2-wheeler transport and other necessities, and meeting community expenses.

Of course, dedicated people with smaller financial resources may also find it possible to settle in the township. Each application is considered individually.

Residing temporarily in Newcomer units...

While waiting for accommodation to be built or to become available, the Newcomer may be lodged in one of the Newcomer units which become available from time to time in various settlements around Auroville. The idea behind this scheme is to make apartments available to Newcomers during their first two years for an appropriate financial contribution, which is reinvested in the maintenance of these units as well as in creating more Newcomer housing.

Alternatively, Newcomers may be able to stay in the residences of established Aurovilians who are out of Auroville for longish periods, such as 6 months or more, against payment of any running expenses or maintenance required on the place.

TO BE A TRUE AUROVILIAN
a guideline statement from The Mother

1. *The first necessity is the inner discovery by which one learns who one really is behind the social, moral, cultural, racial and hereditary appearances. At our inmost centre there is a free being, wide and knowing, who awaits our discovery and who ought to become the acting centre of our being and our life in Auroville.*

2. *One lives in Auroville in order to be free of moral and social conventions; but this liberty must not be a new slavery to the ego, its desires and its ambitions. The fulfilment of desires bars the route to the inner discovery which can only be attained in peace and the transparency of a perfect disinterestedness.*

3. *The Aurovilian must lose the proprietary sense of possession. For our passage in the material world, that which is indispensable to our life and to our action is put at our disposal according to the place we should occupy there. The more conscious our contact is with our inner being, the more exact are the means given.*

4. *Work, even manual work, is an indispensable thing for the inner discovery. If one does not work, if one does not inject his consciousness into matter, the latter will never develop. To let one's consciousness organise a bit of matter by way of one's body is very good. To establish order around oneself helps to bring order within oneself.*

   One should organise life not according to outer, artificial rules, but according to an organised inner consciousness, because if one allows life to drift without imposing the control of a higher consciousness, life becomes inexpressive and irresolute. It is to waste one's time in the sense that matter persists without a conscious utilisation.

5. *The whole earth must prepare itself for the advent of the new species, and Auroville wants to work consciously towards hastening that advent.*

6. *Little by little it will be revealed to us what this new species should be, and meanwhile the best measure to take is to consecrate oneself entirely to the Divine.*

be at home
a place where men of all countries would

Auroville wants to be the first realisation of human unity based on the teaching of Sri Aurobindo, where men of all countries would be at home.

When we ask Aurovilians why they stay in Auroville, it is often difficult for them to elaborate on their choice. Nevertheless, at one time or another we often hear them say, "I feel at home here".

Below is a letter written by an American who visited Auroville in March 1997 for the first time. He knew about the place and its founder, and also knew a number of residents. On his return he wrote about his experience, which is quoted here as a good illustration of the above introductory text of The Mother.

"Since I have come back a few days ago, I have been raving about Auroville like a lovesick madman: I have been to quite a few places, but nowhere have I felt as light, secure, complete and **at home** as I did in Auroville.

"I have never encountered such a concentration of interesting individuals, nor had such a rapid succession of overpowering experiences as I did in the five days I spent in Auroville and the Ashram.

"The goal of my visit was to experience things first-hand, before applying as a newcomer. Well, I arrived, I looked around and I applied immediately! From the first moment I set foot on that red soil, I realized that, for me, Auroville was the only place that made sense, the only adventure worth taking, and the only hope of living out the dreams that have been repressed within me for so long. ...

"Home at last...

Dawn gathering at the Amphitheatre

the ashram
and Auroville

The 'Samadhi' of Sri Aurobindo and The Mother is the centre of the Sri Aurobindo Ashram

When Sri Aurobindo arrived in Pondicherry in 1910 a few associates lived with him, at first as members of his household, then in the neighbourhood. It was only in 1920, after The Mother's arrival, that the numbers began to increase considerably and collective life gradually took on the form of an Ashram. The Mother supervised its activities until her passing in 1973, when it was counting 2,000 members residing in houses scattered around Pondicherry, with 400 students in its school.

Today, the number of residents and students is being held steady through a careful screening process prior to acceptance.

Visitors often ask, what is the relationship between Auroville and the Ashram? The answer is that, while both the Ashram and Auroville were initiated by The Mother under the inspiration of Sri Aurobindo, the two entities are physically and legally separate, and for the past many years have been evolving in an independent way.

The task of giving a concrete form to Sri Aurobindo's vision was entrusted to The Mother.

The creation of a new world, a new humanity, a new society expressing and embodying the new consciousness is the work she has undertaken. By the very nature of things, it is a collective ideal that calls for a collective effort so that it may be realised in terms of an integral human perfection.

The Ashram, essentially founded and built up by The Mother, was the first step towards the accomplishment of this goal. The project of Auroville is the next step, "more exterior", which seeks to widen the base of the endeavour to establish harmony between soul and body, spirit and nature, heaven and earth, in the collective life of mankind.

She also indicated that there is no fundamental difference in the attitude towards the future and the service of the Divine.

The Sri Aurobindo Ashram is a community which aims at providing Sri Aurobindo's and The Mother's disciples with the optimal conditions for living a spiritual life devoted to inner development and transformation.

In Auroville, the emphasis is put not only on the individual development and emergence of a new being, but also on the creation of a new city and a new type of society embodying, in a living manner, an actual human unity in diversity.

sri aurobindo

a pioneer seer

Sri Aurobindo, a scholar...

Sri Aurobindo was born in Calcutta on 15th August 1872. At the age of seven he was sent by his father to England to receive an English education. He was a brilliant student, and his studies – first in London, then at Cambridge – could have enabled him to obtain the highest posts in the Indian Administrative Service. In 1893, at the age of 21, he returned to India and spent 13 years in the administration of the State of Baroda.

...a freedom fighter...

In 1906, he went to Calcutta as Principal of the Bengal National College, and openly joined the movement for the liberation of India, becoming the Bengal leader. He was the first to demand total independence from Britain, rather than an improved form of collaboration.

In 1908, he was accused of sedition and conspiracy and put in prison. This period, which lasted a year, proved to be a turning point for him. He did intensive inner work which led to a number of spiritual experiences. When he left prison, he continued with his political and journalistic work; but soon, in answer to an inner directive, he withdrew from political life.

...and a yogi...

Sri Aurobindo arrived in Pondicherry on 4th April 1910. After four years of silent yoga, he started in 1914 – jointly with The Mother – a philosophical monthly magazine called "The Arya", in which most of his major works were published, namely, "The Life Divine", "The Synthesis of Yoga", "Essays on the Gita", "On the Veda", "The Human Cycle", and "The Ideal of Human Unity".

In 1926 he withdrew from outer contact, though he kept up an extensive correspondence with his disciples. He wrote, among other things, his major literary creation, the epic poem "Savitri – a Legend and a Symbol". During this period, he gave priority to the inner work of calling down a new force, consciousness and light which he called the Supramental, and to his inner transformation. This lasted until his passing away in 1950. He entrusted The Mother with continuing the work he had undertaken.

the mother
a conscious laboratory for a new species

The Mother, a multi-faceted person...
The Mother was born in Paris, France, on 21st February 1878.

While still a child, she spontaneously followed an inner discipline which was accompanied by numerous psychic and spiritual experiences. Growing up, she took much interest in literature and philosophy, and practised painting, music and occultism, for which she had remarkable gifts. She first met Sri Aurobindo in 1914, and at once recognised in him the figure of the great guide of whom she had had repeated visions. Some months later, because of the war, she had to return to France. After a stay in Japan, she came back to Pondicherry in 1920, and never left again.

... who will receive the charge of an Ashram in India...

When, in 1926, Sri Aurobindo withdrew permanently to his room and stopped meeting new people, she took over the material and spiritual charge of the disciples, giving great attention to the physical and spiritual development of each Ashramite as well as to the development of each collective service and commercial unit. The Mother monitored very closely the education of the children who had come with their parents to join the Ashram. She also started an International Centre of Education and put a strong emphasis on daily sports and physical activities meant to strengthen a body submitted to spiritual forces.

During the nineteen-fifties, she held some classes in French for the Ashram children and inmates, in course of which she commented on some of Sri Aurobindo's words and answered questions. The record of these classes was published in several volumes under the title, "Questions and Answers".

... and will explore the body's cellular consciousness...

The Mother withdrew more or less to her room in 1958, and then completely from 1962 onwards, primarily to devote more time to the "yoga of the cells", though she continued to manage the Ashram. She appeared in public, for what is known in India as Darshan, only four times a year. From this period onwards, she had regular conversations on her work and her inner development with a disciple named Satprem, who has published them in 13 volumes titled "Mother's Agenda". From 1965 onwards, she often spoke of Auroville. On 17th November 1973 she left her body.

a new world
has been born

On 29th February 1956, a new force,
which Sri Aurobindo calls the "Supramental Force", manifested in the Earth's physical atmosphere.
Long before, Sri Aurobindo had the knowledge
of its existence and had announced its descent and its physical action.

The following year, The Mother commented on this event to her disciples:

Last year, when I announced to you the manifestation of the Supramental consciousness and light and force, I should have added that it was a forerunner of the birth of a new world. But at that time, the new world was so much engulfed in the ancient that even now there are very few people who are aware of its birth and of the difference it brings into the world. Yet the action of the new forces has continued in a very regular, very persistent, very obstinate and, to a certain extent, very effective way. The result of all that has been noted at every step in almost day to day experiences.

First of all, it is not merely a new conception of the spiritual life and the divine Reality. Sri Aurobindo has expressed this conception in the most clear and complete manner. Briefly it may be formulated somewhat like this.

*The old spirituality was an escape from life towards the divine Reality, leaving the world where it was, as it was. Our new vision, on the contrary, is the divinisation of life, the transformation of the material into a divine world. This has been said, and more or less understood; this indeed is the basic idea of what we want to do. But this work could have been a simple continuation, an amelioration, an enlargement of the world as it was. And the whole conception, however true, however new it may be, so long as it remains in the higher regions, in the domain of pure idea, can be only potentially a new creation. But what has happened is really something new: **a new world has been born**. It is not the old that is being transformed, it is quite a new world that has really concretely been born.*

At the present hour we are in the very heart of a period of transition, where the two are intertwined; the old persists, still all-powerful, and continues to dominate the ordinary consciousness, while the new glides in, still modest, unnoticed to the extent that for the moment it disturbs nothing much externally, and even in the consciousness of most people it is quite imperceptible.

Yet, the road to reach there is a new road, that has never before been traced; none went by that way, none did that. It is a beginning, a universal beginning.

Therefore it is an adventure absolutely unexpected and unforeseeable. There are people who love adventure. I call them and I tell them: I invite you to the great adventure, and in this adventure you are not to repeat spiritually what others have done before us, because our adventure begins from beyond that stage. We are for a new creation, entirely new, carrying in it all the unforeseen, all risks, all hazards, – a true adventure of which the goal is sure victory, but of which the way is unknown and has to be traced out step by step in the unexplored. It is something which has never been in the present universe and will never be in the same manner. If it interests you, well, embark.

What will happen tomorrow, I do not know. You must leave behind whatever has been designed, whatever has been built up, and then march on into the unknown. Come what may.

The working of this force is now felt all over the world. Indeed, if we compare the world as it was in 1956 with how it is today, there is no doubt that the pace of change during the last sixty years, in so many fields, has accelerated enormously.

a cradle
for the new species

On 1st January 1969, thirteen years after this Supramental manifestation, the Mother announced that a new consciousness had descended upon earth. Satprem talks about it in his book, "On the Way to Supermanhood".

"The first wave of this new consciousness is quite visible, it is chaos to perfection, it has seized us without our understanding anything of it, although everywhere we see its flux and reflux. Men have turned errant and aberrant, they have set out in quest of something they do not understand, something that pushes and presses within, they have set out on the way to anything whatever, they have knocked at all doors good and bad, tilted and smashed at walls and windmills; or suddenly overcome by laughter, they have left all, dropped out, and said farewell to the old establishment.

"It is quite natural for this first effect to be aberrant since, by definition, it strays out of the old closed circuit... These supermen-in-the-making*, who do not yet even know themselves, will more than likely be found among the most heterodox elements of society, the so-called good for nothings, the bastards, the refractory of the general prison, the revolting – against-heaven-knows-what except that they know they want it no longer. These are the new crusaders without a crusade, partisans without a party, opposers so very opposed they do not even want any more of the opposition, they want something quite different, without "mores" and "lesses", shades of difference, offensives or defensives, something without "black" or "white", without "good" or "bad", without "yes" or "no", something completely different and completely outside all the wheelings and grindings of the Machine which would like to trap them through their negation if it cannot win their affirmation.

"Or it may be at the other end of the spectrum, these supermen-in-the-making will be found among those who have gone the long road of the mind, its labyrinths, its endless circlings, its answers which answer nothing, which only raise other questions, its solutions which solve nothing... Then they too set out on the way. The rift itself has opened to them the possible...

"What will they do these wanderers, these trans-humans, inhabitants of an as yet non-existent country? At first they will perhaps stop wandering and not stir at all. They have perhaps understood that the change is to be made within, and that if nothing is changed within, nothing will ever be changed outside for centuries and centuries. They will perhaps remain where they are, in that little street, that grey country, in humble disguise and an old routine which will no longer be a routine; for they will do everything with another sight, another sense, another attitude – the inner sense which changes all. And if they persevere, they will realise that this one single spark of true light which they carry within has the power of stealthily, quietly changing everything around them...

"Or... perhaps one day they will feel impelled to rejoin their kind, the new kind; to build with them some living testimony of their aspiration, as others built pyramids or cathedrals... Perhaps a city of the new world?"

* The superman is a "transitional being", he is the preparer of another being on earth, as different from man as we are different from the monkey and perhaps more different, for man is still of the same substance as the monkey, whilst the new being will be of another substance, immortal, luminous and light like Truth itself. He is the forerunner of the "supramental being" announced by Sri Aurobindo, and his substance is the laboratory of a perilous adventure.

28 February 2018
Auroville's 50th Anniversary
The Meditation and Water Ceremony

On the 28th February, as the children carrying the water samples went up the incline leading to the Urn, they came down the other side and moved across the stage to the Golden Disc used as the water receptacle. The water bearers then placed the paper 'drops' with the name of the water source on it at the edge of the stage, and exited, while the Auroville Choir sang 'Earth's

Water is the symbol of a state of consciousness or plane." — Sri Aurobindo

The water ceremony after the early morning meditation of 28th February, 2018 was reminiscent of the soil ceremony that took place on 28th February, 1968. The joining of the waters of the world symbolises unity and the unity of the waters of the world. Water is like the Mother's force, which permeates into every nook and corner of the universe and is there for all.

321 water samples from 77 countries in the world were mixed together

As the water samples arrived from all over the world, they were entered into a chart, while paper cutouts in the shape of water drops were prepared by an Auroville press and then spray painted in blue by an Auroville unit which also provided the paper and made them ready.

Meanwhile, the Auroville schools collaborated in training and preparing the children for the ceremony, while a huge group of volunteers from Auroville and the Ashram organised themselves to receive and guide an expected crowd of 6,000 or mere attendees.

Aspiration Chant' as given by the Mother, and the musicians played inspired music to the large gathering.

We believe that the event of 28th February 2018 was a gift from the Universal Mother to Auroville. She put the idea of a water ceremony into our heads, motivated us to go for it, inspired all who heard about it to bring or send water samples from all over the world, brought together all who were meant to participate in it, galvanised the organisers into action, and finally presided over the whole event to see that everything went smoothly, serenely, beautifully.

Auroville contact information

General information	: info@auroville.org.in	AV International	: avi@auroville.org.in
Guest house booking	: avguests@auroville.org.in	Media Interface	: mediainterface-avf@auroville.org.in
Joining Auroville	: entry@auroville.org.in	**Auroville website**	**: www.auroville.org**

International Publications

Auroville Architecture
by Franz Fassbender

Auroville Form Style and Design
by Franz Fassbender

Landscapes and Gardens of Auroville
by Franz Fassbender

Inauguration of Auroville
by Franz Fassbender

Auroville in a Nutshell
by Tim Wrey

Death doesn't exist
The Mother on Death, Sri Aurobindo on Rebirth
Compiled by Franz Fassbender

Divine Love
Compiled by Franz Fassbender

Five Dream
by Sri Aurobindo

A Vision
Compiled by Franz Fassbender

Passage to More than India
by Dick Batstone

The Mother on Japan
Compiled by Franz Fassbender

Children of Change: A Spiritual Pilgrimage
by Amrit (Howard Shoji Iriyama)

Memories of Auroville - told by early Aurovilians
by Janet Feran

The Journeying Years
by Dianna Bowler

Auroville Reflected
by Bindu Mohanty

Finding the Psychic Being
by Loretta Shartsis

The Teachings of Flowers
The Life and Work of the Mother of the Sri Aurobindo Ashram
by Loretta Shartsis

The Supramental Transformation
by Loretta Shartsis

**The Mother's Yoga - 1956-1973 (English & French)
Vol. 1, 1956-1967 & Vol. 2, 1968-1973**
by Loretta Shartsis

Antithesis of Yoga
by Jocelyn Janaka

Bougainvilleas PROTECTION
by Narad (Richard Eggenberger), Nilisha Mehta

Crossroad The New Humanity
by Paulette Hadnagy

Die Praxis Des Integralen Yoga
by M. P. Pandit

The Way of the Sunlit Path
by William Sullivan

Wildlife great and small of India's Coromandel
by Tim Wrey

A New Education With A Soul
by Marguerite Smithwhite

Featured Titles

Divine Love

The texts presented in this book are selected from the Mother and Sri Aurobindo.

"Awakened to the meaning of my heart. That to feel love and oneness is to live. And this the magic of our golden change, is all the truth I know or seek, O sage."

Sri Aurobindo, Savitri, Book XII, Epilog

A Vision by the Mother

On 28th May 1958, the Mother recounted a vision she once had of a wonderful Being of Love and Consciousness, emanated from the Supreme Origin and projected directly into the Inconscient so that the creation would gradually awaken to the Supramental Consciousness. The Mother's account of this vision was brought out a first time in November 1906, in the Revue Cosmique, a monthly review published in Paris.

A Dream – Aims and Ideals of Auroville
the Mother on Auroville

50 years of Auroville from 28.02.1968 - 28.02.2018

Today, information about Auroville is abundant. Many people try to make meaning out of Auroville – about its conception, to what direction should we grow towards, and, what are we doing here?

But what was Mother's original Dream and what was her Vision for Auroville back then?

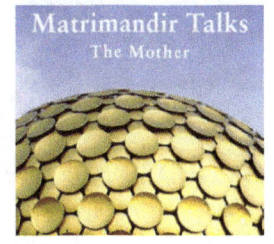

Matrimandir Talks by the Mother

This book presents most of Mother's Matrimandir talks, including how she conceived the idea for this special concentration and meditation building in Auroville.

Memories of Auroville - Told by early Aurovilians

Memories of Auroville is a book about the very early days of Auroville based on interviews made in 1997 with Aurovilians who lived here between 1968 and 1973. The interviews presented in this book are part of a history program for newcomers that I had created with my friend, Philip Melville in 1997. The plan was to divide Auroville's history into different eras and then interview Aurovilians according to their area of knowledge. Our first section would cover the years from 1968 till 1973 when the Mother was still in her physical body.

The Way of the Sunlit Path

May The Way of the Sunlit Path be a convenient guide for activating this ancient truth as a support for a Conscious Evolution.
May it illumine the transformation offered to us in the Integral Yoga.

A Dream Takes Shape (in English, French, Hindi)

A comprehensive brochure on the international township of Auroville in, ranging from its Charter and "Why Auroville?" to the plan of the township, the central Matrimandir, the national pavilions and residences, to working groups, the economy, making visits, how to join, its relationship to the Sri Aurobindo Ashram, and its key role in the future of the world. This brochure endeavours to highlight how The Mother envisioned Auroville from its inception, some of the major achievements realised over the years, and some of the difficulties currently faced in implementing the guidelines which she gave.

Mother on Japan

I had everything to learn in Japan. For four years, from an artistic point of view, I lived from wonder to wonder. And everything in this city, in this country, from beginning to end, gives you the impression of impermanence, of the unexpected, the exceptional... ...everything in this city, in this country, from beginning to end, gives you the impression of impermanence, of the unexpected, the exceptional. You always come to things you did not expect; you want to find them again and they are lost – they have made something else which is equally charming.

Auroville Reflected

On 28 February 1968, on an impoverished plateau on the Coromandel Coast of South India, about 4,000 people from around the world gathered for a most unusual inauguration. Handfuls of soil from the countries of the world were mixed together as a symbol of human unity. Why did Indira Gandhi, the erstwhile Prime Minister of India, support this development for "a city the earth needs?" Why did UNESCO endorse this project? Why does the Dalai Lama continue to be involved in the project? What led anthropologist Margaret Mead to insist that records must be kept of its progress? Why did both historian William Irwin Thompson and United Nations representative Robert Muller note that this social experiment may be a breakthrough for humanity even as critics commented, "it is an impossible dream"?

A House For the Third Millennium
Essays on Matrimandir

Nightwatch at the Matrimandir...
A cosmic spectacle; the black expanse above, the big black crater of Matrimandir's excavation carved deep into the soil. The four pillars - two of which are completed and the other two nearing completion - are four huge ships coming together from the four corners of the earth to meet at this pro propitious spot...

Passage to More than India

This book is a voyage of discovery. In 1959 the author, Dick Batstone, a classically educated bookseller in England, with a Christian background, comes across a life of the great Indian polymath Sri Aurobindo, though a series of apparently fortuitous circumstances. A meeting in Durham, England, leads him to a determination to get to the Sri Aurobindo Ashram in Pondicherry, a former French territory south of Madras.